The Micro-Mastery Method

The Micro-Mastery Method

Matthew Petchinsky

The Micro-Mastery Method: Transform Your Skills in Just Minutes a Day

By: Matthew Petchinsky

Introduction

In a world obsessed with grand achievements and overnight success, it's easy to overlook the transformative power of small, consistent actions. We live in an era where the big picture often overshadows the individual brushstrokes that bring it to life. Yet, history and personal experiences repeatedly reveal that greatness is not built on monumental leaps, but on the accumulation of countless small steps taken consistently over time. This philosophy, though simple, holds the key to unlocking personal growth, mastering skills, and achieving long-term success.

The Power of Small, Consistent Actions

At its core, progress is a series of small victories. Whether you're learning a new language, building a career, or transforming your health, the most effective changes are often those that seem almost insignificant in the moment. It's the choice to dedicate just ten minutes a day to practice, to read one chapter of a book, or to substitute one unhealthy snack for a healthier option. These decisions, repeated consistently, create a powerful ripple effect that compounds over time.

The concept of "small wins" is backed by science. Behavioral psychologists emphasize that breaking down larger goals into manageable tasks reduces overwhelm, increases motivation, and fosters a sense of accomplishment. Every small win builds momentum and reinforces your belief in your ability to achieve more. This sense of momentum is what propels you forward, even when the road seems long or the challenges insurmountable.

Moreover, small, consistent actions align with the way our brains learn and adapt. The brain's neuroplasticity—the ability to form and reorganize synaptic connections—thrives on repetition. Each small action strengthens neural pathways, turning deliberate effort into second nature. Over time, what once felt difficult becomes effortless, and what seemed out of reach becomes part of your reality.

Why Micro-Mastery is the Secret to Learning Faster

In the pursuit of growth and expertise, many people fall into the trap of trying to master everything all at once. This approach often leads to frustration, burnout, and a sense of failure. Enter micro-mastery, a strategy that focuses on breaking down complex skills into smaller, more manageable components. By achieving proficiency in one small area before moving on to the next, you not only learn faster but also gain the confidence to tackle increasingly challenging tasks.

Micro-mastery works because it transforms the overwhelming into the achievable. Consider learning to play the guitar: instead of striving to master the entire instrument immediately, micro-mastery encourages you to start with a single chord, a simple riff, or a favorite song. As you conquer each small piece, you experience a sense of accomplishment that fuels your desire to continue. These bite-sized successes keep you engaged and motivated, turning the learning process into a series of enjoyable milestones.

This approach isn't just limited to hobbies; it applies to any area of life. Want to improve your communication skills? Start by focusing on mastering the art of active listening. Interested in coding? Begin with one basic programming concept or a simple project. Micro-mastery allows you to celebrate progress regularly, which makes the journey to expertise not only faster but also more fulfilling.

Furthermore, micro-mastery taps into the power of focused learning. By narrowing your attention to one small area at a time, you reduce cognitive overload and deepen your understanding of the task at hand. This depth-first approach accelerates skill acquisition and enhances your ability to retain information. The result? You become adept more quickly and with greater confidence.

A Path to Sustainable Growth

Small, consistent actions and micro-mastery are not just strategies for learning or self-improvement—they are tools for building a life rooted in resilience and growth. Together, they create a framework that makes even the most daunting goals feel approachable. They remind us that success isn't about perfection or speed but about persistence and intention.

As you embark on this journey, remember that every small step you take is a step closer to your goal. Each moment of micro-mastery, each incremental improvement, is a testament to your commitment to growth. By embracing the power of small, consistent actions and the art of micro-mastery, you're not only learning faster but also creating a foundation for a life of continuous progress and achievement. The path may not always be easy, but it is always worth it. And it begins, as all great things do, with one small step.

Chapter 1: The Micro-Mastery Mindset

In a world that often celebrates perfection and instant success, shifting to a mindset focused on progress over flawlessness can feel counterintuitive. Yet, this shift is essential for anyone seeking lasting growth and mastery. At the heart of this transformation is the concept of micro-mastery—a powerful framework for skill acquisition and personal development that emphasizes breaking down complex goals into manageable, actionable tasks. By adopting the micro-mastery mindset, you can reframe your approach to learning, overcome the paralysis of perfectionism, and unlock your potential.

Shifting from Perfectionism to Progress

Perfectionism is often hailed as a desirable trait, a mark of ambition and high standards. However, the reality is that perfectionism frequently paralyzes us, turning challenges into insurmountable obstacles. When perfection is the goal, the fear of making mistakes can lead to procrastination or abandonment of the effort altogether. The result is stagnation, frustration, and a lack of progress.

The micro-mastery mindset offers a liberating alternative: focus on progress instead of perfection. It's about celebrating incremental improvements and understanding that mastery is a journey, not a destination. Here's how to make the shift:

1. **Redefine Success**: Instead of viewing success as flawless execution, redefine it as consistent effort and measurable improvement. Each small step you take, no matter how imperfect, brings you closer to your goal.

2. **Embrace Mistakes as Learning Opportunities**: Mistakes are not failures; they are valuable feedback. Each misstep teaches you what doesn't work and guides you toward what does. By reframing mistakes as part of the process, you can approach challenges with curiosity rather than fear.

3. **Adopt a Beginner's Mindset**: The micro-mastery mindset thrives on the idea that every expert was once a beginner. By approaching each task with humility and openness, you create space for genuine learning and growth.

4. **Celebrate Small Wins**: Progress often goes unnoticed when you're focused solely on the end goal. Take time to acknowledge and celebrate each milestone, no matter how small. These victories fuel motivation and reinforce your commitment.

By shifting from perfectionism to progress, you free yourself to take action, experiment, and grow. This mindset lays the foundation for micro-mastery, enabling you to break down complex skills into manageable pieces and achieve consistent, meaningful progress.

How to Break Down Any Skill into Micro-Tasks

At the heart of the micro-mastery mindset is the ability to break down complex skills into micro-tasks—small, focused actions that are achievable and repeatable. This approach not only makes learning more manageable but also accelerates the path to competence. Here's how to do it:

1. **Define the Big Picture**

   Start by identifying the overarching skill or goal you want to achieve. Be specific. Instead of saying, "I want to play the guitar," say, "I want to play my favorite song on the guitar." A clear vision of the end goal provides direction and purpose.

2. **Identify the Core Components**

   Break the skill into its fundamental elements. For example, playing a song on the guitar might involve:
      - Learning basic chords
      - Practicing chord transitions
      - Mastering strumming patterns
      - Building finger strength and dexterity
      - Playing the song slowly and accurately

3. **Create Micro-Tasks**

   For each core component, create micro-tasks that focus on specific, actionable steps. These tasks should be small enough to complete in a short session, ideally 10–30 minutes. Using the guitar example:
      - Practice the G chord for 10 minutes
      - Transition between G and C chords 20 times

- ◦ Strum down-up patterns slowly for 5 minutes
- ◦ Play the first line of the song at half speed

4. **Sequence the Tasks**

Arrange the micro-tasks in a logical sequence that builds on previous steps. Start with foundational skills and gradually progress to more advanced tasks. This ensures that each step feels achievable and prepares you for the next.

5. **Set Realistic Goals**

Establish clear, attainable goals for each session. Instead of aiming for perfection, aim for improvement. For instance, your goal might be to transition smoothly between two chords 10 times, even if you make occasional mistakes.

6. **Track Your Progress**

Keep a record of your efforts and achievements. Tracking progress not only provides a sense of accomplishment but also helps you identify areas that need more attention. This feedback loop is essential for continuous improvement.

7. **Adjust and Iterate**

Learning is not a linear process. As you work through your micro-tasks, be prepared to adjust your approach. If a particular task feels too difficult, break it down further or spend more time practicing. Flexibility is key to sustaining progress.

The Benefits of Micro-Mastery

Breaking down skills into micro-tasks offers several distinct advantages:

- **Reduces Overwhelm**: Complex goals can feel daunting, but micro-tasks make them approachable. Instead of climbing a mountain in one leap, you take it step by step.
- **Builds Momentum**: Each completed task fuels your confidence and motivation, making it easier to tackle the next challenge.
- **Enhances Focus**: By concentrating on one small task at a time, you reduce distractions and deepen your learning.
- **Accelerates Learning**: Micro-mastery allows you to quickly identify and address weak points, enabling faster progress.
- **Encourages Consistency**: Small tasks are easier to fit into your daily routine, fostering the habit of regular practice.

Putting the Micro-Mastery Mindset into Action

To adopt the micro-mastery mindset, start with a skill or goal you've been struggling to achieve. Break it down using the steps outlined above, and commit to consistent practice. Remember, the journey to mastery is not about grand gestures or perfect performance—it's about showing up, making progress, and celebrating each small win along the way.

As you embrace this approach, you'll discover that no goal is too ambitious, no skill too complex. With the micro-mastery mindset, you have the tools to learn faster, achieve more, and build a life of continuous growth and achievement. It's time to stop chasing perfection and start making progress—one micro-task at a time.

Chapter 2: The 15-Minute Framework

Time is one of our most valuable resources, yet in our busy lives, finding large chunks of time for learning or self-improvement can feel impossible. Enter the 15-Minute Framework—a simple, effective method for structuring short, focused learning sessions that maximize productivity and accelerate progress. By dedicating just 15 minutes a day, you can create meaningful momentum toward mastering skills, achieving goals, and unlocking your potential.

How to Structure Short Learning Sessions

The key to the 15-Minute Framework is intentionality. It's not just about setting aside 15 minutes—it's about using that time effectively. To do this, you need a structured approach that minimizes distractions, optimizes focus, and aligns with your long-term goals. Here's how to structure a productive 15-minute session:

1. Set a Clear Intention

- Start each session by identifying what you want to achieve in those 15 minutes. This could be mastering a specific skill, practicing a technique, or reviewing what you've learned. Clarity ensures that every minute is spent with purpose.
- Example: Instead of saying, "I'll practice guitar," say, "I'll practice transitioning between the G and C chords smoothly."

2. Break the Time into Segments

Divide the 15 minutes into smaller segments to maintain focus and engagement. A common structure is:

- **1-2 minutes for warm-up or review**: Begin with a quick activity to get into the right mindset or refresh your memory.
- **10-12 minutes of focused work**: Dedicate the majority of the time to the task at hand, staying fully engaged.
- **1-2 minutes for reflection**: End the session by reviewing what you accomplished and noting any challenges or successes.

This segmentation helps prevent burnout and ensures that every session feels productive and complete.

3. Eliminate Distractions

- Create a learning environment that minimizes interruptions. Turn off notifications, close unnecessary tabs or apps, and let others know you're unavailable for the next 15 minutes.
- Use tools like timers or focus apps to help you stay on track.

4. Incorporate Micro-Goals

- Each session should have a small, specific goal that contributes to your larger objective. Micro-goals provide a clear target and a sense of accomplishment when achieved.
- Example: "Today, I'll memorize three new vocabulary words in Spanish."

5. Leverage Active Learning

- Active learning techniques, such as practicing, problem-solving, or teaching others, are far more effective than passive activities like reading or watching videos. Engage directly with the material to deepen your understanding and retention.

6. Track Your Progress

- Use a notebook, app, or journal to record what you worked on and how you felt about the session. This helps you monitor your improvement over time and identify areas for further focus.

Examples for Mastering Skills in Less Time

The 15-Minute Framework can be applied to virtually any skill. Below are specific examples of how to use this method effectively for a variety of pursuits:

1. Learning a New Language

- **Warm-Up (1-2 minutes)**: Review vocabulary flashcards or a quick grammar rule.
- **Focused Work (10-12 minutes)**:
    - Practice speaking a new sentence out loud.
    - Write a short paragraph using recently learned words.
    - Listen to a short audio clip and jot down key phrases.
- **Reflection (1-2 minutes)**: Note which words or concepts were challenging and plan to revisit them later.

2. Playing a Musical Instrument

- **Warm-Up (1-2 minutes)**: Play scales or simple exercises to loosen up your fingers.
- **Focused Work (10-12 minutes)**:
    - Practice one section of a song slowly and with precision.
    - Work on a specific technique, such as fingerpicking or bowing.
    - Use a metronome to improve timing on a challenging passage.
- **Reflection (1-2 minutes)**: Identify improvements or areas that need more attention.

3. Writing and Content Creation

- **Warm-Up (1-2 minutes)**: Review your outline or brainstorm ideas.
- **Focused Work (10-12 minutes)**:
    - Write the opening paragraph of a blog post or chapter.
    - Edit a specific section of your work for clarity and flow.
    - Generate three new ideas for future content.
- **Reflection (1-2 minutes)**: Assess how the writing flowed and plan what to tackle next.

4. Fitness and Physical Skills

- **Warm-Up (1-2 minutes)**: Perform light stretching or a few basic movements.
- **Focused Work (10-12 minutes)**:
    - Practice a specific yoga pose or sequence.
    - Perform a set of bodyweight exercises, focusing on form.
    - Work on improving one aspect of a sport, such as dribbling in basketball.
- **Reflection (1-2 minutes)**: Note how your body feels and set a goal for the next session.

5. Professional Skills

- **Warm-Up (1-2 minutes)**: Review key points from a recent meeting or tutorial.
- **Focused Work (10-12 minutes)**:
    - Practice a presentation for an upcoming project.
    - Learn one new feature in a software program you use.
    - Draft a professional email or memo with attention to tone and clarity.

- **Reflection (1-2 minutes)**: Evaluate what you accomplished and plan how to build on it.

The Science Behind the Framework

The effectiveness of the 15-Minute Framework is supported by cognitive and psychological research:

- **The Pomodoro Technique**: Studies show that short bursts of focused work, like the 15-minute sessions in this framework, improve concentration and reduce mental fatigue.
- **The Spacing Effect**: Short, regular learning sessions promote better retention and understanding compared to cramming information all at once.
- **Flow State Activation**: Fifteen minutes of focused effort can often lead to a state of flow, where you become deeply immersed in the task and achieve peak productivity.

Making the Most of Your 15 Minutes

To truly benefit from the 15-Minute Framework, consistency is key. While each session may feel small in isolation, the cumulative effect is profound. Over time, these focused bursts of effort create significant progress and momentum, proving that mastery doesn't require hours of effort—it requires intention, discipline, and the willingness to start.

By adopting this framework, you'll discover that 15 minutes a day is enough to make meaningful strides in any area of life. It's not about how much time you have; it's about how you use the time you've got. So grab your timer, set your intention, and take the first step toward mastering your next skill—15 minutes at a time.

Chapter 3: Momentum Over Motivation

One of the biggest misconceptions about achieving goals is that motivation is the key to success. While motivation can ignite action, it is notoriously unreliable. It ebbs and flows, often deserting us when we need it most. Instead of relying on fleeting bursts of inspiration, the real secret lies in building momentum—a self-sustaining force that drives consistent action regardless of how motivated you feel on any given day. This chapter explores how to stay consistent without relying on willpower and how tracking progress becomes a powerful tool for maintaining that momentum over the long term.

Staying Consistent Without Relying on Willpower

Willpower, like motivation, is a finite resource. Research has shown that the more decisions we make or tasks we perform throughout the day, the more our willpower depletes, leaving us vulnerable to procrastination and distraction. To overcome this limitation, you need to create systems and habits that make consistency automatic, minimizing your dependence on willpower. Here's how:

1. Build Habits Through Routine

- The key to consistency is turning your desired actions into habits. Habits operate on autopilot, requiring little to no conscious effort once they are established. To build a habit:
    - **Start small**: Commit to an action so small it's impossible to fail, like practicing a skill for just five minutes.
    - **Anchor it to an existing routine**: Pair your new habit with something you already do regularly. For example, practice mindfulness right after brushing your teeth or stretch while waiting for your coffee to brew.
    - **Be consistent**: Perform the action at the same time and place each day. Consistency is more important than intensity in the beginning.

2. Create an Environment That Encourages Success

- Your surroundings play a significant role in shaping your behavior. Design your environment to make your desired actions easy and unavoidable:
    - **Remove friction**: Keep your tools or resources readily accessible. If you want to read more, place books in your living spaces. If you're learning an instrument, leave it within easy reach.
    - **Eliminate distractions**: Identify and minimize sources of distraction that compete for your attention, like turning off notifications during focused sessions.
    - **Use visual cues**: Create reminders of your goals, such as sticky notes, vision boards, or habit trackers, to keep your aspirations front and center.

3. Rely on Discipline, Not Feelings

- While emotions fluctuate, discipline provides a steady foundation for action. Develop the mindset that you will show up and perform the task regardless of how you feel. A simple mantra like "Action first, motivation later" can help you push through moments of reluctance.

4. Leverage Accountability

- Sharing your goals with others or working alongside a partner can keep you consistent. Knowing someone else is counting on you or observing your progress adds an extra layer of motivation.
    - Join a group or community centered around your goal.
    - Use social media to publicly commit to your plans.
    - Partner with a friend for mutual accountability.

5. Use Rewards to Reinforce Behavior

- Positive reinforcement can solidify habits. Reward yourself for completing tasks, especially in the early stages of building momentum.
    - Rewards don't have to be extravagant—they can be as simple as taking a short break, enjoying a favorite snack, or indulging in a hobby.

Tracking Progress to Stay Motivated

Momentum is easier to sustain when you can see tangible evidence of your efforts paying off. Tracking your progress provides this evidence, creating a feedback loop that fuels motivation and encourages continued action. Here's how to effectively track your progress:

1. Choose the Right Metrics

- Track metrics that are meaningful and directly tied to your goals. These can be qualitative (e.g., how you feel about your progress) or quantitative (e.g., the number of tasks completed). Examples include:
    - Time spent practicing a skill.
    - Milestones reached, such as mastering a specific technique.
    - Numerical achievements, like weight lost or money saved.

2. Use Simple Tracking Tools

- You don't need elaborate systems to track progress. Choose tools that are easy to use and integrate seamlessly into your routine:
    - **Journals**: Keep a daily or weekly log of your activities and reflections.
    - **Habit trackers**: Use apps or printable charts to mark off days when you've completed your task.
    - **Calendars**: Mark your progress on a physical or digital calendar to create a visual chain of consistency.

3. Visualize Your Growth

- Seeing your progress in a visual format can be incredibly motivating. Graphs, charts, or even simple streak trackers can illustrate how far you've come and inspire you to keep going.

4. Celebrate Milestones

- Recognize and celebrate small wins along the way. Milestones serve as checkpoints, reminding you of your achievements and the progress you've made. This positive reinforcement keeps you engaged and excited about the journey ahead.

5. Reflect and Adjust

- Periodically review your progress to assess what's working and what isn't. Use these reflections to refine your approach and set new, achievable goals. Reflection not only highlights your growth but also helps you stay aligned with your larger objectives.

Momentum: The Self-Sustaining Engine

When you prioritize momentum over motivation, you create a self-sustaining cycle of action and achievement. Each small step forward builds confidence, reinforces your commitment, and makes the next step easier. Over time, this momentum grows, propelling you toward your goals with minimal effort.

Consider this analogy: motivation is like a match—it can spark the fire, but it burns out quickly. Momentum, on the other hand, is the steady warmth of a well-maintained fire. Once it's burning, it requires only small inputs to keep going.

The Long-Term Benefits of Momentum Over Motivation

1. **Resilience**: Momentum helps you push through challenges and setbacks because you've built a foundation of consistent effort.
2. **Sustainability**: Unlike motivation, which is unpredictable, momentum ensures steady progress over the long term.
3. **Confidence**: Seeing consistent progress reinforces your belief in your ability to achieve your goals.
4. **Efficiency**: By focusing on action rather than waiting for motivation, you make better use of your time and energy.

Putting It All Together

Staying consistent without relying on willpower and tracking your progress to stay motivated are the cornerstones of building momentum. When you combine disciplined habits with visible evidence of your growth, you create a powerful force that carries you forward, even on days when motivation is absent.

By prioritizing momentum over motivation, you're not just taking steps toward your goals—you're transforming the way you approach challenges and opportunities in every area of your life. So start small, track your wins, and let the power of momentum lead you to success.

Chapter 4: The Feedback Loop Advantage

Mastery of any skill is not a straight line but a winding path filled with adjustments, refinements, and continual improvement. At the heart of this journey lies the feedback loop—a process of receiving, analyzing, and applying feedback to refine your skills and progress more effectively. In this chapter, we'll explore how to harness the power of quick feedback to improve your performance and understand when and how to adjust your learning process to stay on track.

Understanding the Feedback Loop

A feedback loop consists of three essential stages:

1. **Action**: You engage in a specific task or practice, applying your current knowledge and skills.
2. **Feedback**: You receive information about your performance, either from an external source (e.g., a mentor, peer, or tool) or through self-assessment.
3. **Adjustment**: You use the feedback to make changes or improvements in your approach before repeating the process.

This iterative cycle accelerates learning by highlighting what works, what doesn't, and how you can improve. Unlike traditional learning methods that emphasize passive absorption of information, feedback loops prioritize active engagement and continual refinement.

Using Quick Feedback to Refine Your Skills

Quick feedback is essential for maintaining momentum and making timely adjustments. Here's how to incorporate feedback into your learning process:

1. Seek Immediate Feedback

- Timely feedback is far more effective than delayed feedback because it allows you to correct mistakes and solidify improvements while the experience is still fresh in your mind. For example:
  - In sports, reviewing game footage right after a practice session highlights areas for improvement.
  - In writing, revisiting your draft immediately after completion helps identify inconsistencies or errors.
  - In coding, debugging as you write ensures you catch and fix issues before they compound.

2. Leverage External Sources

- While self-assessment is valuable, external feedback often provides insights you may overlook. Engage with:
  - **Mentors or Coaches**: Experts can offer targeted advice and highlight subtle areas for refinement.
  - **Peers or Colleagues**: Collaborators can provide diverse perspectives on your work or performance.
  - **Tools and Technology**: Apps, software, and other resources can analyze your performance objectively, such as language-learning apps that track pronunciation or fitness trackers that measure progress.

3. Adopt a Growth Mindset

- Feedback, especially when critical, can feel uncomfortable. Embrace it as a tool for growth rather than a judgment of your abilities. A growth mindset allows you to view challenges as opportunities to improve rather than as setbacks.

4. Focus on Specifics

- General feedback like "good job" or "try harder" is less helpful than specific feedback that identifies precise areas for improvement. For example:
    - Instead of "You need to play better," specific feedback might be, "Work on transitioning from the G to C chord more smoothly."
    - Instead of "Your essay is unclear," feedback might be, "Your thesis statement needs to be more concise."

5. Iterate and Test

- After applying feedback, test the results to see if your adjustments lead to measurable improvement. If the change works, incorporate it into your routine. If not, refine further until you achieve the desired outcome.

When and How to Adjust Your Learning Process

Feedback isn't just about refining individual skills; it's also about evaluating and improving your overall approach to learning. Here's how to know when adjustments are needed and what changes to make:

1. Identify Plateaus

- Plateaus are periods when progress slows or stalls despite continued effort. They are a natural part of the learning process but signal that your current methods may need tweaking.
    - **Signs of a Plateau**: Repeating the same mistakes, lack of noticeable improvement, or feeling bored or unchallenged.
    - **Adjustment Strategy**: Change your routine, introduce new challenges, or focus on a different aspect of the skill to reengage your brain and body.

2. Analyze Feedback Trends

- Look for patterns in the feedback you receive. Repeated suggestions or criticisms indicate recurring issues that require attention.
    - For example, if multiple people point out weak transitions in your writing, prioritize practicing transitions in your next sessions.

3. Experiment with New Techniques

- Sticking to a single approach can limit your growth. Experiment with alternative methods or tools to discover what works best for you.
    - Example: If traditional note-taking isn't effective, try mind-mapping or audio recording your thoughts.
    - Example: If your fitness routine feels stagnant, incorporate interval training or a new workout style.

4. Adjust Your Goals

- Sometimes, the issue lies not in your approach but in your objectives. If your goals are too ambitious or vague, refine them to be more specific, achievable, and time-bound. Use the SMART goal framework:
    - **Specific**: Clearly define what you want to achieve.
    - **Measurable**: Establish criteria to track your progress.
    - **Achievable**: Set realistic goals based on your current abilities.
    - **Relevant**: Align your goals with your overall purpose or interests.
    - **Time-Bound**: Set a deadline to create urgency and focus.

5. Monitor Your Engagement Levels

- If you find yourself losing interest or motivation, it may be time to adjust your approach. Inject variety, gamify your practice, or revisit why the skill matters to you.

Examples of the Feedback Loop in Action

1. **Public Speaking**
   - **Action**: Deliver a speech to a small group.
   - **Feedback**: Receive input on pacing, tone, and body language.
   - **Adjustment**: Practice slowing down your speech and incorporating gestures. Re-deliver the speech to test improvements.

2. **Learning a Language**
   - **Action**: Have a short conversation with a native speaker.
   - **Feedback**: Notice which phrases are misunderstood or corrected.
   - **Adjustment**: Practice pronunciation or grammar rules for those phrases. Repeat the conversation later.

3. **Fitness Training**
   - **Action**: Perform a set of squats during a workout.
   - **Feedback**: Use a mirror or trainer to assess your form.
   - **Adjustment**: Focus on keeping your knees aligned and your back straight. Perform the exercise again with the new focus.

Benefits of the Feedback Loop Advantage

1. **Accelerates Learning**: By addressing mistakes immediately, you avoid reinforcing bad habits and make faster progress.
2. **Increases Confidence**: Regular feedback helps you see tangible improvement, boosting your self-belief.
3. **Enhances Problem-Solving**: The feedback loop trains you to analyze situations critically and adapt effectively.
4. **Promotes Resilience**: Learning to embrace and apply feedback builds mental toughness and perseverance.

Putting It All Together

The feedback loop is a powerful tool for refining your skills and optimizing your learning process. By embracing quick feedback, actively seeking improvement opportunities, and knowing when and how to adjust your methods, you can transform challenges into stepping stones for success.

Remember, mastery is not about perfection—it's about progress. The feedback loop keeps you grounded in the reality of your growth, empowering you to adapt, evolve, and excel in any endeavor. Each iteration of the loop brings you one step closer to your goals, turning the pursuit of mastery into a rewarding, lifelong journey.

Chapter 5: Mastering the Meta-Skill of Learning

Learning is often seen as a process tied to specific tasks or knowledge areas, such as acquiring a new language, playing an instrument, or mastering a profession. However, the ability to learn itself is a skill—a meta-skill—that, when honed, unlocks limitless potential. Mastering the meta-skill of learning enables you to adapt, grow, and thrive in any area of life. This chapter explores how to apply the principles of micro-mastery across all domains and cultivate a mindset of continuous improvement and adaptability.

Applying Micro-Mastery to All Areas of Life

Micro-mastery is not confined to hobbies or academic pursuits; it is a universal approach to skill-building that can be applied to personal growth, relationships, work, and beyond. By breaking down complex challenges into smaller, manageable tasks, you can make progress in any area, no matter how daunting it may initially seem.

1. Career Development

- **Problem**: Career advancement often feels overwhelming, with demands to acquire new skills, meet expectations, and outperform peers.
- **Micro-Mastery Approach**: Identify the specific skills that will have the most significant impact on your role or aspirations. For example:
    - Master the art of effective email communication by learning one principle at a time, such as concise subject lines or clear calls to action.
    - Break down public speaking into micro-tasks: practicing posture, learning to modulate tone, or mastering one presentation at a time.

- Tackle one software tool or feature instead of trying to learn an entire program in one sitting.

By focusing on micro-tasks, you build confidence and expertise incrementally, making it easier to handle larger challenges.

2. Relationships

- **Problem**: Building and maintaining meaningful relationships can seem complex and emotionally taxing.
- **Micro-Mastery Approach**: Break down relational skills into smaller steps:
  - Practice active listening during one conversation a day.
  - Focus on expressing gratitude to one person each week.
  - Learn to manage conflict by addressing small disagreements with empathy and clarity.

These small, intentional actions strengthen your relationships over time, transforming the way you connect with others.

3. Health and Fitness

- **Problem**: Starting or maintaining a fitness journey can feel intimidating, especially with ambitious goals like weight loss or running a marathon.
- **Micro-Mastery Approach**: Apply small, consistent actions to build momentum:
  - Begin with a 10-minute daily walk or a single set of an exercise.
  - Focus on drinking one extra glass of water a day.
  - Swap one unhealthy snack for a healthier option.

Each micro-task builds the foundation for larger lifestyle changes, making long-term goals achievable.

4. Personal Development

- **Problem**: Improving self-awareness, emotional intelligence, or productivity often feels like a lifelong challenge with no clear starting point.
- **Micro-Mastery Approach**:
    - Spend five minutes a day journaling your thoughts or emotions.
    - Reflect on one aspect of your day that could have been handled better and brainstorm alternatives.
    - Implement one productivity hack, such as time-blocking your schedule or decluttering your workspace.

These small, deliberate efforts create a ripple effect that enhances your overall personal growth.

How to Continuously Improve and Adapt

Mastering the meta-skill of learning requires more than just applying micro-mastery to different areas of life. It also involves cultivating a mindset of continuous improvement and adaptability, enabling you to stay relevant and effective in a rapidly changing world. Here's how to do it:

1. Adopt a Growth Mindset

- A growth mindset, as coined by psychologist Carol Dweck, is the belief that abilities can be developed through effort and practice. To cultivate this mindset:
    - Embrace challenges as opportunities to grow.
    - View failure as feedback, not as a reflection of your worth.
    - Celebrate progress, no matter how small.

With a growth mindset, you approach learning as an ongoing journey rather than a finite destination.

2. Become a Lifelong Learner

- The world is constantly evolving, and staying stagnant can lead to obsolescence. Commit to lifelong learning by:
    - Regularly exploring new interests or hobbies.
    - Staying curious and asking questions about the world around you.
    - Reading widely, not just in your area of expertise, but across disciplines.

Lifelong learners are adaptable, innovative, and resilient in the face of change.

3. Embrace the Power of Reflection

- Reflection is a critical component of improvement. Regularly assess your progress and learning experiences to identify strengths, weaknesses, and opportunities for growth.
    - After completing a task, ask yourself: What worked? What didn't? What could I do differently next time?
    - Use a journal or habit tracker to document your reflections and identify patterns over time.

4. Experiment with New Approaches

- Adaptability requires a willingness to step outside your comfort zone and try new methods:
    - Experiment with different learning styles (visual, auditory, kinesthetic) to find what works best for you.
    - Test various tools or resources, such as apps, books, or workshops, to enhance your learning experience.
    - Explore interdisciplinary approaches by combining knowledge from different fields to solve problems creatively.

Experimentation not only expands your skill set but also keeps the learning process engaging and dynamic.

5. Leverage Technology and Tools

- Technology offers countless opportunities to enhance your learning process. Use apps, online courses, and other digital tools to:
    - Track your progress and set goals.
    - Access high-quality learning resources.
    - Connect with mentors, peers, or communities that share your interests.

Staying updated with technological advancements ensures you remain competitive and resourceful.

6. Cultivate Resilience

- Continuous improvement requires resilience—the ability to bounce back from setbacks and keep going. Build resilience by:
  - ◦ Reframing failures as stepping stones to success.
  - ◦ Practicing self-compassion when progress feels slow.
  - ◦ Surrounding yourself with a supportive network of friends, family, or colleagues.

Resilience transforms obstacles into opportunities for growth.

Examples of Applying the Meta-Skill of Learning

1. **Adapting to Career Changes**
   - ◦ Transitioning to a new role or industry can be daunting. By mastering the meta-skill of learning, you can quickly identify the core competencies required, break them into manageable tasks, and apply micro-mastery to gain proficiency.
2. **Navigating Personal Transitions**
   - ◦ Life changes, such as moving to a new city or becoming a parent, demand adaptability. By embracing learning as a skill, you can approach these transitions with confidence and curiosity, continually refining your approach.
3. **Thriving in the Digital Age**
   - ◦ As technology evolves, so do the skills required to stay competitive. Mastering the meta-skill of learning ensures you can quickly adapt to new tools, platforms, or workflows, keeping you ahead of the curve.

The Ripple Effect of Mastering Learning

When you master the meta-skill of learning, the benefits extend beyond individual achievements:

- **Increased Confidence**: The ability to learn anything gives you confidence in your ability to tackle new challenges.
- **Enhanced Creativity**: A broad and adaptable skill set fosters innovative thinking and problem-solving.
- **Stronger Relationships**: By applying micro-mastery to communication and empathy, you build deeper and more meaningful connections with others.
- **A Fulfilling Life**: Lifelong learning keeps you engaged, curious, and open to new experiences, making life richer and more rewarding.

Conclusion: The Power of the Meta-Skill

Mastering the meta-skill of learning is the ultimate key to success in an ever-changing world. By applying micro-mastery to all areas of life and cultivating a mindset of continuous improvement, you can adapt to new challenges, achieve your goals, and unlock your full potential.

The beauty of this approach is that it creates a self-sustaining cycle of growth. Each skill you master makes it easier to learn the next, creating a compounding effect that accelerates your progress. Whether in your career, relationships, or personal development, the ability to learn effectively and adapt is a superpower that will serve you for a lifetime. It all begins with a single step—so start today and watch the ripple effects transform your life.

Appendix A: A 30-Day Micro-Mastery Planner for Any Skill

This 30-day planner is designed to help you achieve focused, incremental progress in mastering any skill using the principles of micro-mastery. By breaking your goal into small, actionable steps and committing to daily practice, you can build momentum, track your progress, and see measurable results in just one month. The planner provides a structure for setting clear objectives, defining micro-tasks, and incorporating feedback and reflection.

How to Use This Planner

1. **Choose a Skill**: Select a skill you want to focus on for the next 30 days. Be specific about what you aim to achieve within this time frame.
   - Example: Instead of "learn guitar," choose "play my favorite song on guitar."
2. **Break It Down**: Divide the skill into smaller components or tasks. Focus on one area each week, building on previous progress.
3. **Set Micro-Goals**: Create small, actionable daily goals that align with your larger objective.
4. **Track Your Progress**: Use this planner to record your daily activities, observations, and reflections. Celebrate small wins along the way.
5. **Incorporate Feedback**: Regularly review your performance and adjust your approach as needed.

Week 1: Building the Foundation

Focus: Understand the basics and set up a foundation for learning.

Day	Task	Notes/Reflection
1	Define your 30-day goal and break it into smaller components.	Example: Learn basic chords (G, C, D) for guitar.
2	Gather resources (tools, tutorials, books) and set up your practice space.	Ensure you have everything needed to start effectively.
3	Learn the first basic concept or skill.	Example: Practice the G chord for 10 minutes.
4	Continue practicing the first skill and evaluate your progress.	Focus on consistency and accuracy.
5	Learn a second basic concept or skill.	Example: Add the C chord to your practice.
6	Combine the first and second skills in a short session.	Example: Transition between G and C chords.
7	Review and reflect on Week 1 progress. Identify challenges.	What worked well? What needs improvement?

Week 2: Expanding and Connecting

Focus: Build on foundational skills by connecting components and adding complexity.

Day	Task	Notes/Reflection
8	Practice Week 1 skills with increased focus on transitions.	Example: Smooth transitions between chords.
9	Introduce a third basic concept or skill.	Example: Learn the D chord.
10	Practice combining all three concepts.	Example: Transition between G, C, and D chords.
11	Focus on improving speed and fluidity.	Example: Use a metronome to maintain rhythm.
12	Attempt a simple exercise that integrates all learned skills.	Example: Play a short chord progression.
13	Record yourself or seek feedback from a mentor or peer.	Note areas for improvement.
14	Reflect on Week 2 progress and adjust your plan as needed.	Celebrate small victories and refine your focus.

Week 3: Deepening Understanding

Focus: Dive deeper into technique and introduce intermediate concepts.

Day	Task	Notes/Reflection
15	Revisit foundational skills and refine technique.	Example: Ensure accuracy and consistency in chords.
16	Learn an intermediate concept or technique.	Example: Practice a basic strumming pattern.
17	Combine intermediate and foundational skills in practice.	Example: Strum while transitioning chords.
18	Focus on a challenging area identified in previous feedback.	Example: Work on smoother chord transitions.
19	Attempt a short exercise or piece that incorporates all learned skills.	Example: Play the first line of a simple song.
20	Record your progress and evaluate changes since Day 1.	Reflect on noticeable improvements.

Day	Task	Notes/Reflection
21	Reflect on Week 3 progress and fine-tune your approach.	Identify strengths and areas needing more focus.

Week 4: Mastery and Application

Focus: Consolidate skills, refine performance, and apply learning in a meaningful way.

Day	Task	Notes/Reflection
22	Practice all concepts learned so far, focusing on fluidity.	Example: Play a full chord progression with rhythm.
23	Add a new layer of complexity or nuance to your practice.	Example: Introduce dynamics or variations in strumming.
24	Attempt a complete exercise or piece.	Example: Play the full song at a slow tempo.
25	Seek external feedback on your performance.	Incorporate suggestions into your practice.
26	Focus on perfecting weak areas identified in feedback.	Example: Work on timing or difficult transitions.
27	Record a final version of your chosen task or piece.	Example: Play the song at full tempo and evaluate performance.
28	Reflect on the entire learning journey. What worked? What didn't?	Summarize your experience and key takeaways.

Day	Task	Notes/Reflection
29	Plan your next steps for continued improvement.	Set a new goal or expand on the current skill.
30	Celebrate your 30-day achievement!	Reflect on how far you've come and share your success with others.

Tips for Success

- **Consistency is Key**: Even if you can't dedicate a full 30 minutes, a consistent 10-15 minutes daily practice yields results.
- **Adapt as Needed**: This planner is a guideline; feel free to adjust tasks based on your specific needs and progress.
- **Seek Feedback Regularly**: External perspectives can highlight areas you might miss and help you improve faster.
- **Celebrate Progress**: Recognize and reward yourself for small victories to stay motivated.

By following this 30-day planner, you'll not only make measurable progress in your chosen skill but also develop the discipline and confidence to tackle new challenges using the principles of micro-mastery.

<u>Message from the Author:</u>

I hope you enjoyed this book, I love astrology and knew there was not a book such as this out on the shelf. I love metaphysical items as well. Please check out my other books:

-Life of Government Benefits

-My life of Hell

-My life with Hydrocephalus

-Red Sky

-World Domination:Woman's rule

-World Domination:Woman's Rule 2: The War

-Life and Banishment of Apophis: book 1

-The Kidney Friendly Diet

-The Ultimate Hemp Cookbook

-Creating a Dispensary(legally)

-Cleanliness throughout life: the importance of showering from childhood to adulthood.

-Strong Roots: The Risks of Overcoddling children

-Hemp Horoscopes: Cosmic Insights and Earthly Healing

- Celestial Hemp Navigating the Zodiac: Through the Green Cosmos

-Astrological Hemp: Aligning The Stars with Earth's Ancient Herb

-The Astrological Guide to Hemp: Stars, Signs, and Sacred Leaves

-Green Growth: Innovative Marketing Strategies for your Hemp Products and Dispensary

-Cosmic Cannabis

-Astrological Munchies

-Henry The Hemp

-Zodiacal Roots: The Astrological Soul Of Hemp

- Green Constellations: Intersection of Hemp and Zodiac

-Hemp in The Houses: An astrological Adventure Through The Cannabis Galaxy

-Galactic Ganja Guide

Heavenly Hemp

Zodiac Leaves

Doctor Who Astrology

Cannastrology

Stellar Satvias and Cosmic Indicas

Celestial Cannabis: A Zodiac Journey

AstroHerbology: The Sky and The Soil: Volume 1

AstroHerbology:Celestial Cannabis:Volume 2

Cosmic Cannabis Cultivation

The Starry Guide to Herbal Harmony: Volume 1

The Starry Guide to Herbal Harmony: Cannabis Universe: Volume 2

Yugioh Astrology: Astrological Guide to Deck, Duels and more

Nightmare Mansion: Echoes of The Abyss

Nightmare Mansion 2: Legacy of Shadows

Nightmare Mansion 3: Shadows of the Forgotten

Nightmare Mansion 4: Echoes of the Damned

The Life and Banishment of Apophis: Book 2

Nightmare Mansion: Halls of Despair

Healing with Herb: Cannabis and Hydrocephalus

Planetary Pot: Aligning with Astrological Herbs: Volume 1

Fast Track to Freedom: 30 Days to Financial Independence Using AI, Assets, and Agile Hustles

Cosmic Hemp Pathways

How to Become Financially Free in 30 Days: 10,000 Paths to Prosperity

Zodiacal Herbage: Astrological Insights: Volume 1

Nightmare Mansion: Whispers in the Walls

The Daleks Invade Atlantis

Henry the hemp and Hydrocephalus

10X The Kidney Friendly Diet
Cannabis Universe: Adult coloring book
Hemp Astrology: The Healing Power of the Stars
Zodiacal Herbage: Astrological Insights: Cannabis Universe: Volume 2
<u>Planetary Pot: Aligning with Astrological Herbs: Cannabis Universes: Volume 2</u>
Doctor Who Meets the Replicators and SG-1: The Ultimate Battle for Survival
Nightmare Mansion: Curse of the Blood Moon
<u>The Celestial Stoner: A Guide to the Zodiac</u>
Cosmic Pleasures: Sex Toy Astrology for Every Sign
Hydrocephalus Astrology: Navigating the Stars and Healing Waters
Lapis and the Mischievous Chocolate Bar

Celestial Positions: Sexual Astrology for Every Sign
Apophis's Shadow Work Journal: : A Journey of Self-Discovery and Healing
Kinky Cosmos: Sexual Kink Astrology for Every Sign
Digital Cosmos: The Astrological Digimon Compendium
Stellar Seeds: The Cosmic Guide to Growing with Astrology
Apophis's Daily Gratitude Journal

Cat Astrology: Feline Mysteries of the Cosmos
The Cosmic Kama Sutra: An Astrological Guide to Sexual Positions
Unleash Your Potential: A Guided Journal Powered by AI Insights
Whispers of the Enchanted Grove

Cosmic Pleasures: An Astrological Guide to Sexual Kinks
369, 12 Manifestation Journal

Whisper of the nocturne journal(blank journal for writing or drawing)

The Boogey Book

Locked In Reflection: A Chastity Journey Through Locktober

Generating Wealth Quickly:

How to Generate $100,000 in 24 Hours

Star Magic: Harness the Power of the Universe

The Flatulence Chronicles: A Fart Journal for Self-Discovery

The Doctor and The Death Moth

Seize the Day: A Personal Seizure Tracking Journal

The Ultimate Boogeyman Safari: A Journey into the Boogie World and Beyond

Whispers of Samhain: 1,000 Spells of Love, Luck, and Lunar Magic: Samhain Spell Book

Apophis's guides:

Witch's Spellbook Crafting Guide for Halloween

<u>Frost & Flame: The Enchanted Yule Grimoire of 1000 Winter Spells</u>

<u>The Ultimate Boogey Goo Guide & Spooky Activities for Halloween Fun</u>

Harmony of the Scales: A Libra's Spellcraft for Balance and Beauty

The Enchanted Advent: 36 Days of Christmas Wonders

Nightmare Mansion: The Labyrinth of Screams

Harvest of Enchantment: 1,000 Spells of Gratitude, Love, and Fortune for Thanksgiving

The Boogey Chronicles: A Journal of Nightly Encounters and Shadowy Secrets

The 12 Days of Financial Freedom: A Step-by-Step Christmas Countdown to Transform Your Finances

Sigil of the Eternal Spiral Blank Journal

A Christmas Feast: Timeless Recipes for Every Meal

Cosmic Sales: The Astrological Guide to Black Friday Shopping
Legends of the Corn Mother and Other Harvest Myths
Whispers of the Harvest: The Corn Mother's Journal
The Evergreen Spellbook
The Doctor Meets the Boogeyman
The White Witch of Rose Hall's SpellBook
The Gingerbread Golem's Shadow: A Study in Sweet Darkness
The Gingerbread Golem Codex: An Academic Exploration of Sweet Myths
The Gingerbread Golem Grimoire: Sweet Magicks and Spells for the Festive Witch
The Curse of the Gingerbread Golem
10-minute Christmas Crafts for kids
<u>Christmas Crisis Solutions: The Ultimate Last-Minute Survival Guide</u>
Gingerbread Golem Recipes: Holiday Treats with a Magical Twist
The Infinite Key: Unlocking Mystical Secrets of the Ages
Enchanted Yule: A Wiccan and Pagan Guide to a Magical and Memorable Season
Dinosaurs of Power: Unlocking Ancient Magick
Astro-Dinos: The Cosmic Guide to Prehistoric Wisdom
Gallifrey's Yule Logs: A Festive Doctor Who Cookbook
The Dino Grimoire: Secrets of Prehistoric Magick
The Gift They Never Knew They Needed
The Gingerbread Golem's Culinary Alchemy: Enchanting Recipes for a Sweetly Dark Feast
A Time Lord Christmas: Holiday Adventures with the Doctor
Krampusproofing Your Home: Defensive Strategies for Yule
Silent Frights: A Collection of Christmas Creepypastas to Chill Your Bones
Santa Raptor's Jolly Carnage: A Dino-Claus Christmas Tale
Prehistoric Palettes: A Dino Wicca Coloring Journey
The Christmas Wishkeeper Chronicles

If you want solar for your home go here: https://www.harborso-lar.live/apophisenterprises/

Get Some Tarot cards: https://www.makeplayingcards.com/sell/
apophis-occult-shop

Get some shirts: https://www.bonfire.com/store/apophis-shirt-emporium/

<u>Instagrams:</u>
@apophis_enterprises,
@apophisbookemporium,
@apophisscardshop
Twitter: @apophisenterpr1
 Tiktok:@apophisenterprise
Youtube: @sg1fan23477, @FiresideRetreatKingdom
Hive: @sg1fan23477
CheeLee: @SG1fan23477

Podcast: Apophis Chat Zone: https://open.spotify.com/show/5zXbrCLEV2xzCp8ybrfHsk?si=fb4d4fdbdce44dec

Newsletter: https://apophiss-newsletter-27c897.beehiiv.com/

If you want to support me or see posts of other projects that I have come over to: **buymeacoffee.com/mpetchinskg**
I post there daily several times a day

Get your Dinowicca or Christmas themed digital products, especially Santa Raptor songs and other musics. Here: **https://sg1fan23477.gumroad.com**

Apophis Yuletide Digital has not only digital Christmas items, but it will have all things with Dinowicca as well as other Digital products.